INCREDIBLE 3D
EYE TRICKS

INCREDIBLE 3D
EYE TRICKS

GENE LEVINE & GARY W. PRIESTER

Creative Advisor: Brad Honeycutt

ARCTURUS

ARCTURUS

This edition published in 2012 by Arcturus Publishing Limited
26/27 Bickels Yard, 151–153 Bermondsey Street,
London SE1 3HA

ISBN: 978-1-84858-030-5
AD002272EN

Printed in Singapore

Contents

Stereogram Scenes

A 'Scene Stereogram' is either a 3D stereogram framed by 2D elements or a 3D stereogram framing one or more 2D elements.

The traditional stereogram is presented with the least visual distraction possible. The 3D effect comes from the brain and eyes integrating two or more vertical columns of pattern or objects and, if there is any imagery not in synch with this, there will be visual dissonance. So why on earth deliberately introduce large, distracting 2D elements into a 3D stereogram?

Well, despite the danger of disruption, 2D pictures can make even the most simple of stereograms more intriguing and, at the same time, the stereogram gives 2D subject matter quite a lift. This complementary visual play presents stereogram content more dynamically than the traditional stereogram and provides a fresh challenge to stereogram aficionados who think they have seen it all.

ALL STEREOGRAMS IN THIS BOOK are meant to be viewed using parallel or divergent vision. Mixing 2D with the 3D may trigger some common stereogram viewing problems. The two most likely problems would be unintentionally viewing cross-eyed or viewing with double fusion.

Cross-eyed viewing will have the opposite effect of what is intended. 3D objects that should be popping out will look as if they are going inward or inside out. See the viewing tips in this book (pages 8–9) if you are having trouble keeping your eye-lines apart.

Whether they involve pattern or objects, stereograms are created from multiple repeats of vertical columns or panels. If the viewer's vision compares two columns against two columns it is called double fusion. The effect of double fusion is doubled objects floating on top of one another with clipped sides. The best way to deal with the double-fusion problem is to move your face closer, effectively increasing the parallax between your eyes.

Parallax is a critical factor when viewing any kind of stereogram. With stereograms, parallax refers to the spacing between the vertical repeats that make up a stereo image. Too wide makes for difficulty and possible eyestrain; too narrow and double fusion may occur. Combining very wide parallax and very narrow parallax within a single stereogram creates hyper-stereo. Hyper-stereo creates a more profound 3D depth, but is more challenging to view.

There is a simple way to control parallax problems: move the stereo image closer or farther from your face. Move back for too wide and move forward for too narrow. Imagine that you are looking at a poster-sized stereogram.

If you stand too close, the parallax will be impossibly wide to view correctly. If viewed from a distance, things will fall into place as intended. An optimal distance is generally determined by pure instinct and the unconscious practice you have experienced viewing the world since you were an infant.

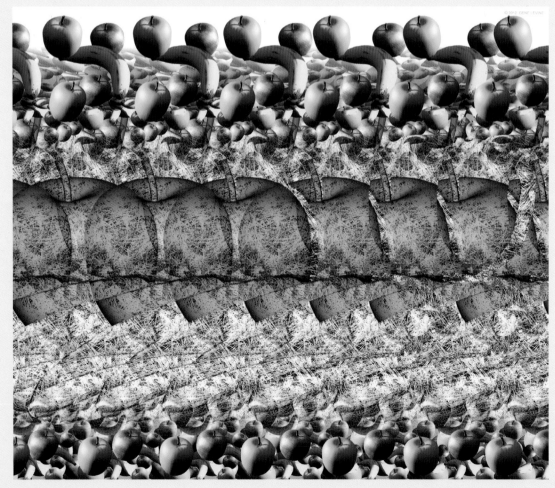

Reveal on page 105

IT HAS BEEN ARGUED that early cave-dwelling artists were aware of the 3D properties of divergent vision. However, the technical inability to repeat a pattern with any precision makes this doubtful. The earliest example of stereo image repetition was probably the Great Ziggurat of Ur erected in the 21st century BCE by the Sumerians. Though the original decor has long worn away, the multi-tiered structural patterns leave little doubt that not all artisans or acolytes could have been unaware of its magical 3D properties.

Viewed as real magic, ancient stereogram imagery carried the value of rare spice and even precious metals. A golden arc – its outside engraved with repeating cuneiform and inside containing the very first beginnings of a nascent 3D algorithm – was sent by Zoroastrian priests as a blessing and gesture of goodwill to the Egyptian Court around the 12th dynasty.

No record of stereo vision is recorded in Western civilization until Alexander the Great invaded Egypt and stumbled on to mysterious divergent-vision hieroglyphs spread across the lost tomb walls of Pharaoh Stereopsisis. The hieroglyphs were closely studied by Alexander's mathematicians, Demetrius, Diametrious and Deximeter. They further refined the original algorithm and invented a mythological explanation for what was referred to as the vision of the Gods.

Nine centuries later, Luthgarde, a member of the Optomecian Monk Order, rediscovered manuscripts of the Greek mathematicians and referred to them in his journal as the Three Ds. A few centuries later, a young Galileo, inspired by Luthgarde's journal, applied its mystic meanderings to a more practical theory, producing what can be considered the first true stereogram algorithm. Though the general view is that the Church had Galileo arrested for postulating a heliocentric world, in reality it was the parallel viewing of crude stereogram images that got him imprisoned for using what the Pope called 'demon vision'.

Papal condemnation and the two-dimensional emphasis of Renaissance art forms kept stereogram art latent until the advent of Modern Art between the two World Wars. Stereograms were just gaining public attention when the Second World War broke out.

After the Nazis occupied Paris, they declared stereograms a degenerative Bolshevik art form and immediately destroyed all algorithms from the Sorbonne's Stereogram Department. They ultimately confiscated all European stereogram art and stacked it outside the Sacre Sirds Cathedral, setting it ablaze in what came to be known as the Night of the Interesting Fire. Parisians, staring aghast into the flames, swore they saw the Four Horsemen of the Apocalypse materialize within as a 3D hidden-image.

An Italian janitor working at the Sorbonne managed to smuggle out the one remaining algorithm, which had escaped detection, disguised as a tapestry of pure random pattern. It was handed over to the victorious Allies as soon as hostilities ended and was shipped to America, where it lay dormant and unappreciated for 50 years until recognized by an entrepreneur who happened to be a computer genius. Thanks to modern media and the personal computer, stereograms were about to become the rage of the 1990s.

By taking stereograms from ancient curiosity into the new age, Gene Levine and Gary Priester, known as the 2Gs of 3D, have become the most advanced practitioners of this art. The images contained within this book are the latest chapter in an ancient saga of magic.

Viewing tips

How to view autostereograms

IF YOU ARE VIEWING stereograms for the first time, the effect will probably not be obvious. Some people see them right away, but it is more usual to spend some time learning first how to view them. Once you learn the technique, a whole new world will open up before your eyes. This is intended as a guide for viewers who have never seen stereogram 3D effects, and for those who may be a bit rusty.

Please don't be discouraged if you can't visualize the effects right away. After all, what you are doing is overcoming a lifetime habit of viewing everything with 'normal' stereovision: that which gives us a sense of depth in our everyday viewing of the world. (Fig.1, right)

First, let's try a visual aid. After that come practices for viewing without aid.

By placing a bit of cardboard between your eyes (Fig. 2) you cannot use normal, or cross-eyed vision. Instead, you are forced into parallel vision, which is just what we need to bring out the 3D in a stereogram.

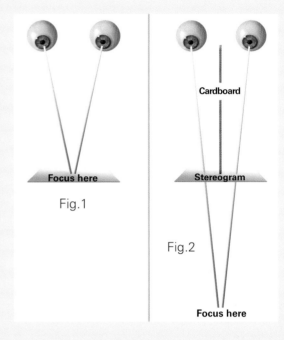

Fig.1

Fig.2

Illustrated above is a piece of cardboard with a cut-out for nose and glasses, but just a simple bit of cardboard will do.

Unlike cross-eyed vision, there is no strain or discomfort with parallel vision. The key, in fact, is to relax your eyes into viewing this way.

Below is a stereo-pair image. Place the cardboard directly in the middle of the pair, as illustrated in Fig. 2. Now place the other end of the cardboard between your eyes. Forget focusing, for now.

If alignment is good, you should see only one image. Now relax your eyes and slowly bring things into focus, pulling your head back. Remember, there will be no doubt when you see a 3D effect – you will know it for sure. When you are sure, hold that focus and remove the cardboard. You should now see three images, the one in the middle containing the 3D effects. Congratulations, you are now viewing an autostereogram (a stereogram that works without physical aids) as it should be seen.

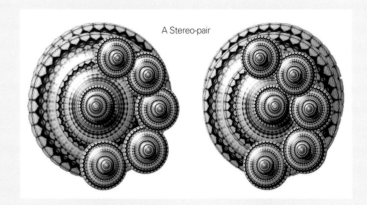

A Stereo-pair

Below are practices without aids, called 'freeviewing'. *The secret is to let go of the normal way you focus on something on a page. Let the eyes relax.*

Practice # 1

o   o

Is that it? Two zeros?

What you want to do here is have your mind process these two objects until they appear as three. Let the eyes relax, and move your head forward or away until three zeros appear clearly.

Your first inclination is to focus on the above two objects as is normal. But now, look behind them; look behind the page and forget about focusing. Try this for a while until you gradually see three zeros.

When you see a non-existent object appear between the two existing ones, you have mastered the basis of the Stereo-Pair. It is the centre object where the 3D effect takes place. This is the crux of autostereograms.

So where does that centre image come from?

It is helpful to remember that visual perception happens within the brain – not the eyes. What we're doing here is fooling the brain. The eyes are feeding it visual information as usual, but not in the usual manner. The mind gives us a middle object. And if you introduce some subtle offsets and distortions into two otherwise similar objects, the mind will perceive depth even though it is not truly there.

Practice # 2

o   o   o

If you view three objects as an autostereogram, you should perceive four objects. Four objects will look as if there are five, etc. etc.

Practice # 3

And now for some 3D.

Between these two objects, another object should appear with the smaller square floating over the larger.

Practice # 4
Still can't see it?

Pull back, and focus normally on the central object of the three, below. Now lean *slowly* forward into the screen holding that focus until it is broken or you see four objects, clearly.

Master these practices, and you should have no problem moving on to fully fledged stereograms.

747 Emerging

view this way

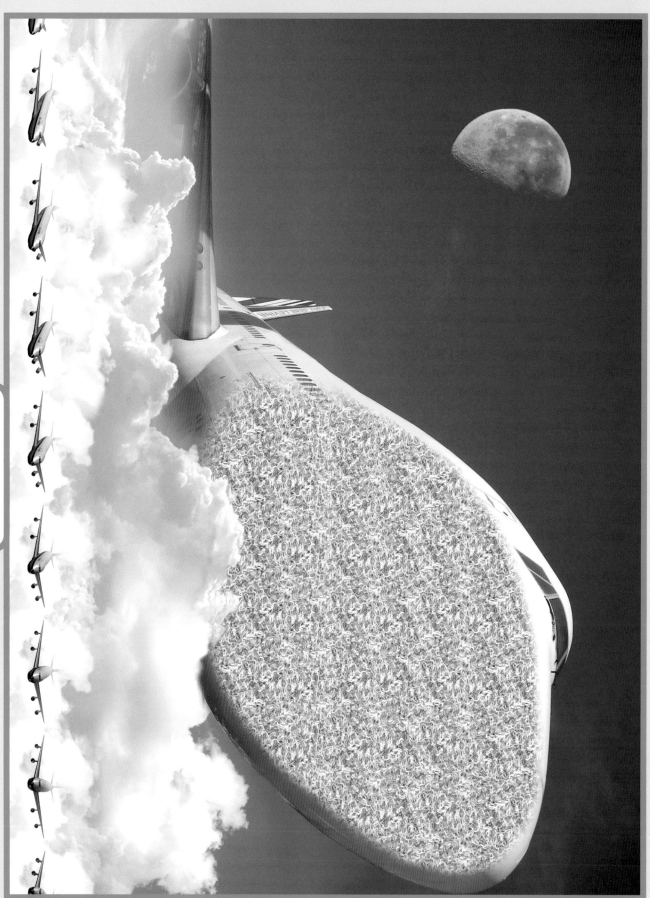

view this way

Green Man

view this way

view this way

At Last

view this way

THE PYRAMIDS

Pyramid. The lowest chamber cut into the bedrock upon which the pyramid was built and was unfinished. The so-called Queen's Chamber and King's Chamber are higher up within the pyramid structure. The Great Pyramid of Giza is the only pyramid in Egypt known to contain both ascending and descending passages. The main part of the Giza complex is a setting of buildings that included two mortuary temples in honor of Khufu (one close to the pyramid and one near the Nile), three smaller pyramids for. The Great Pyramid of Giza is the only pyramid in Egypt known to contain both ascending and descending passages. The main part of the Giza complex is a se...

view this way

Lawn Chair

view this way

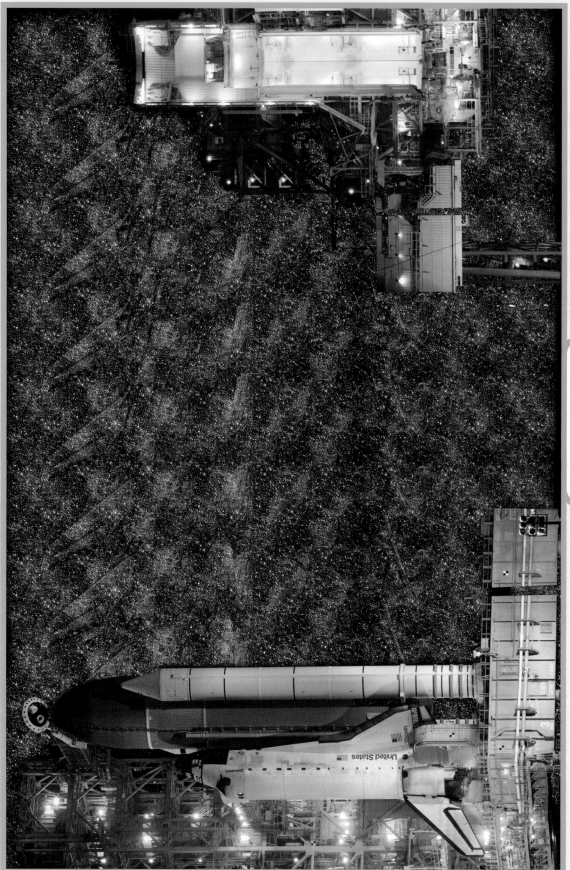

view this way

view this way

Magical Cube

view this way

view this way

view this way

view this way

view this way

Blue Cove

view this way

view this way

Medicine Cabinet

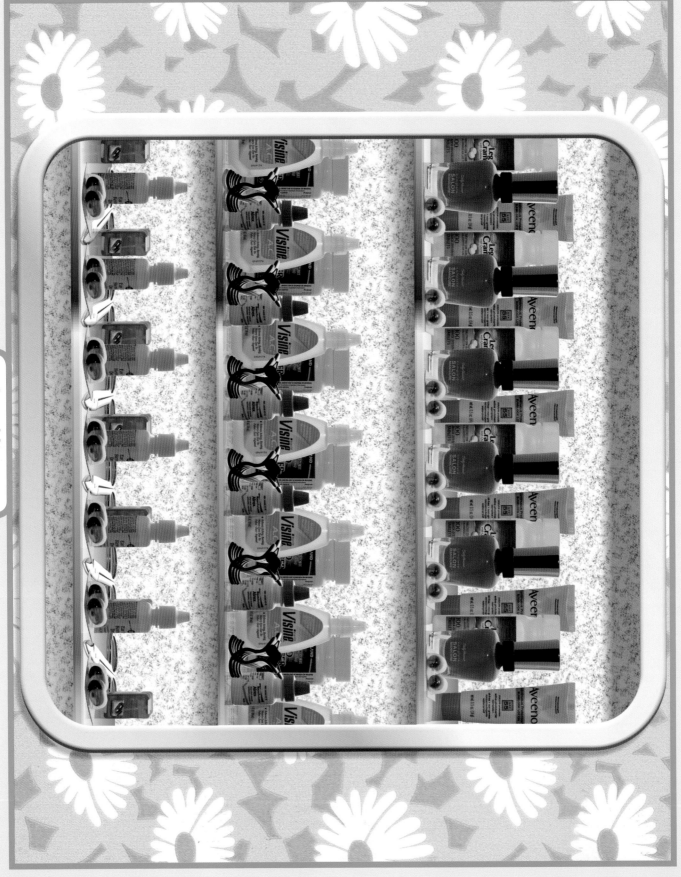

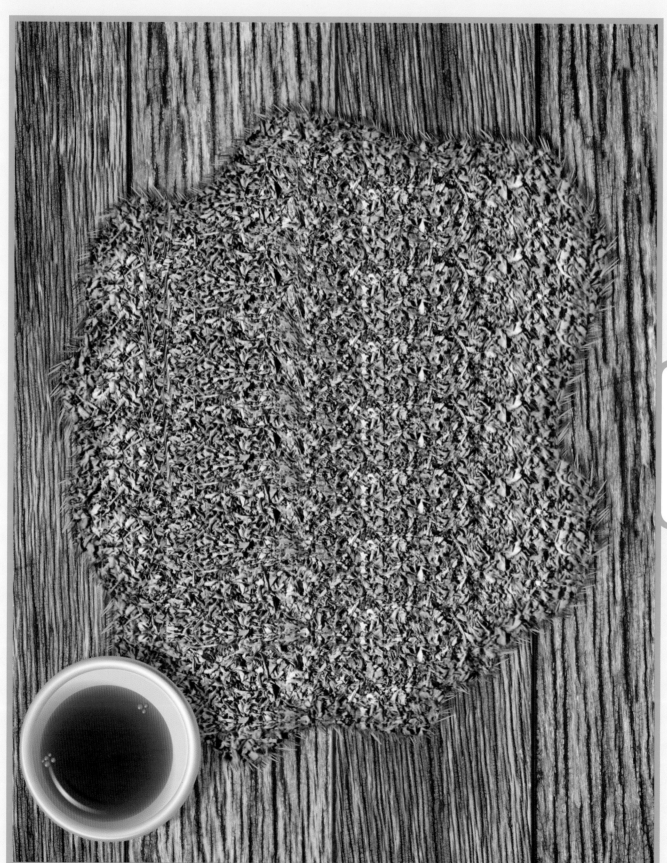

view this way

Dragon Wings

view this way

view this way

view this way

Snow People

view this way

view this way

view this way

view this way

Sandbox

view this way

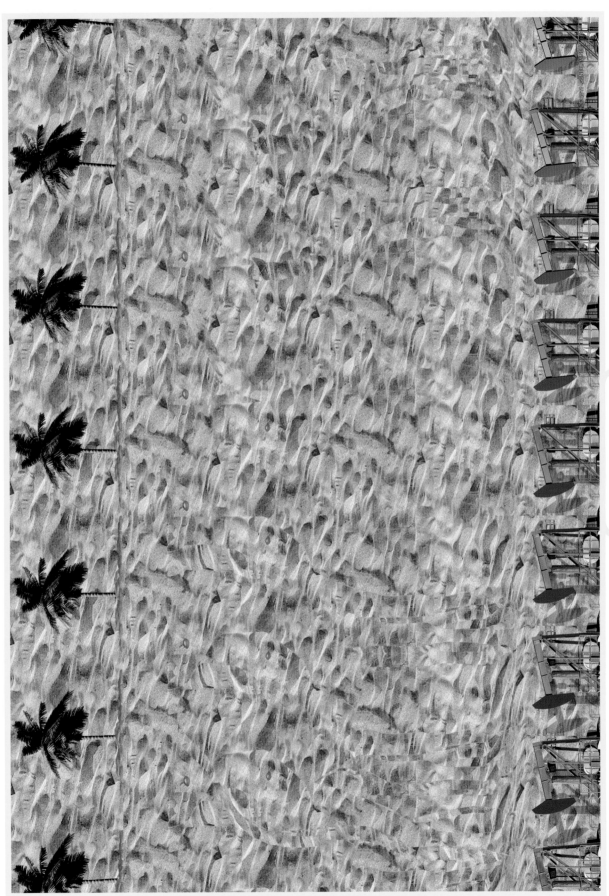

view this way

Skateboarder

view this way

view this way

Snowscreen

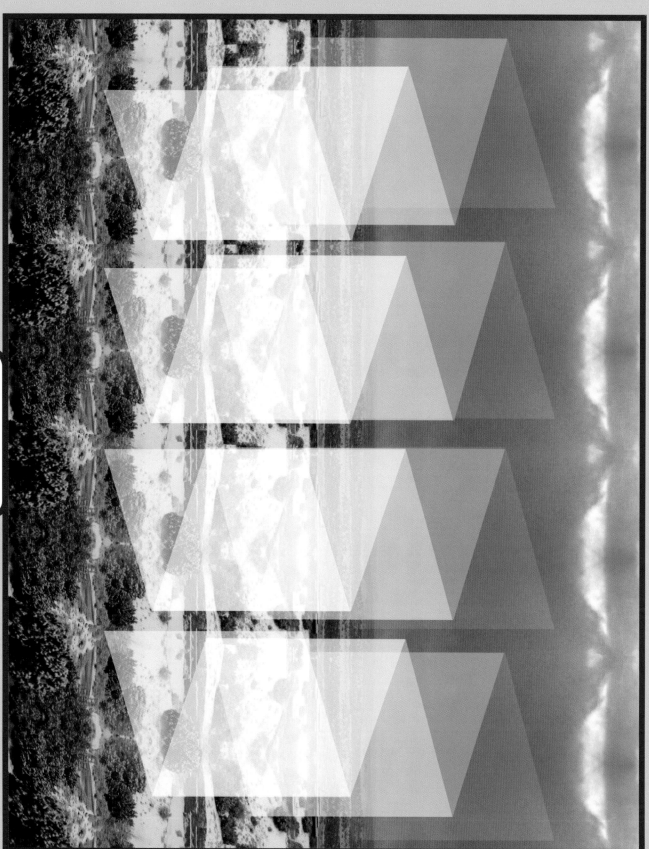

view this way

view this way

Field Compass

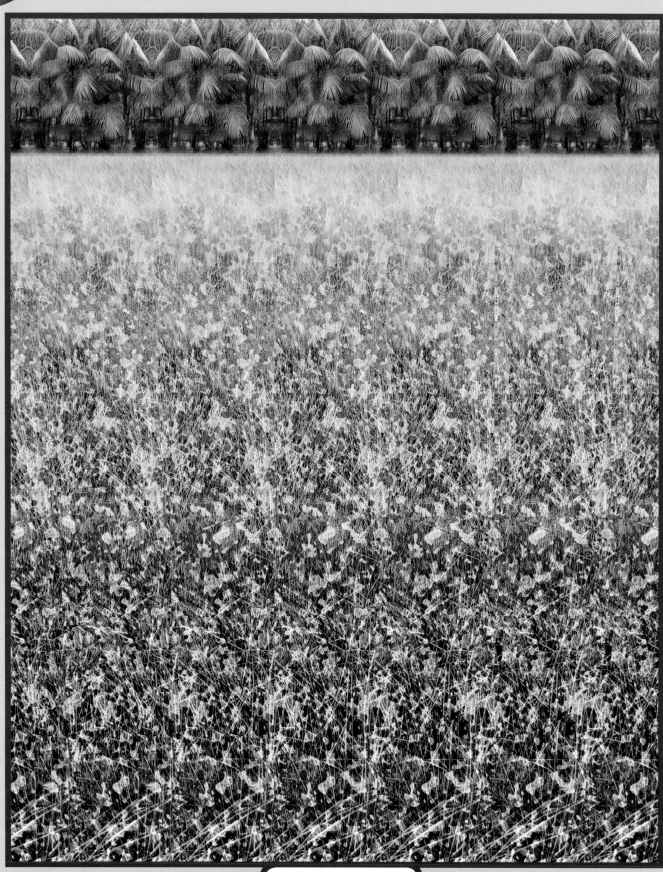

view this way

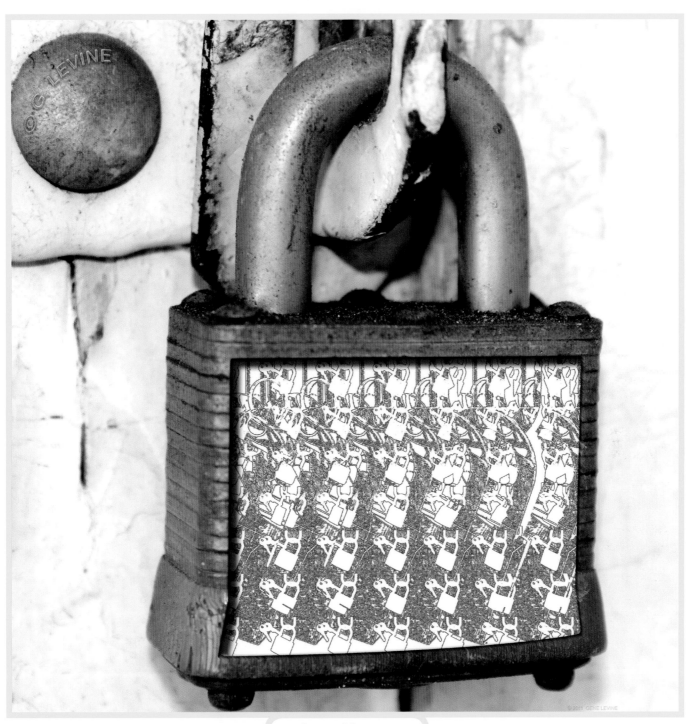

view this way

Tea Pot

view this way

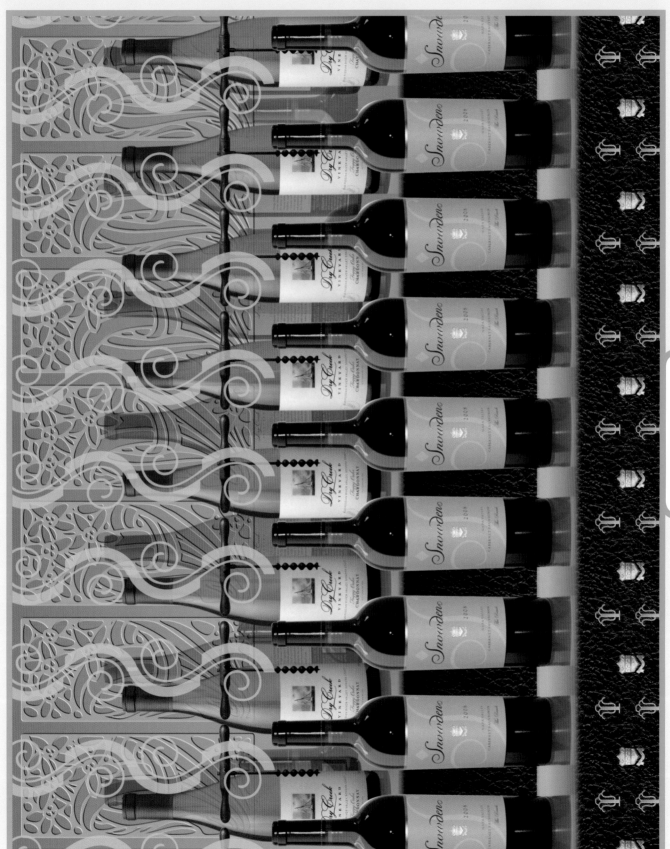

view this way

Fossil Mountain

view this way

view this way

Underwater Danger

view this way

view this way

Yellow Hills

view this way

view this way

view this way

view this way

Wine Barrel

view this way

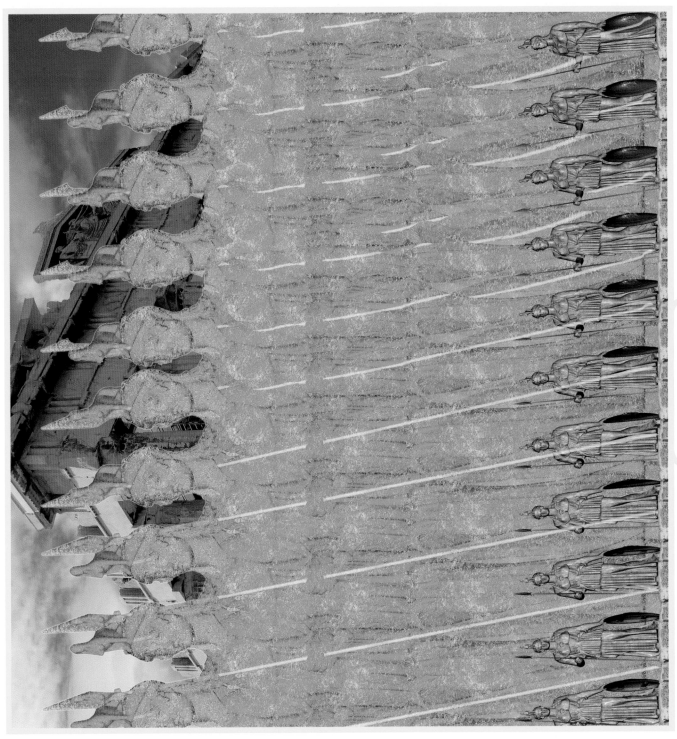

view this way

Sands of Time

view this way

view this way

Jack

view this way

view this way

Flamingo Park

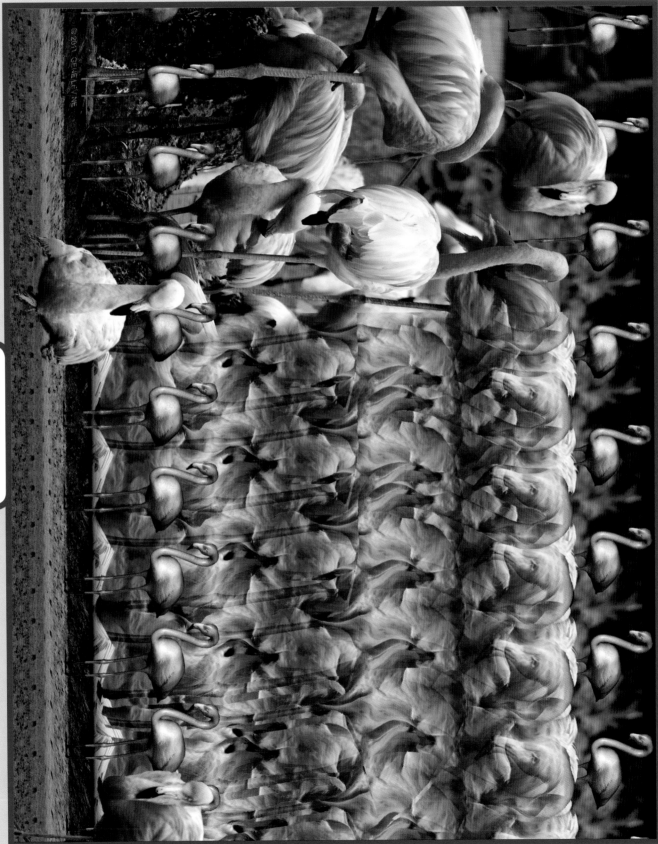

view this way

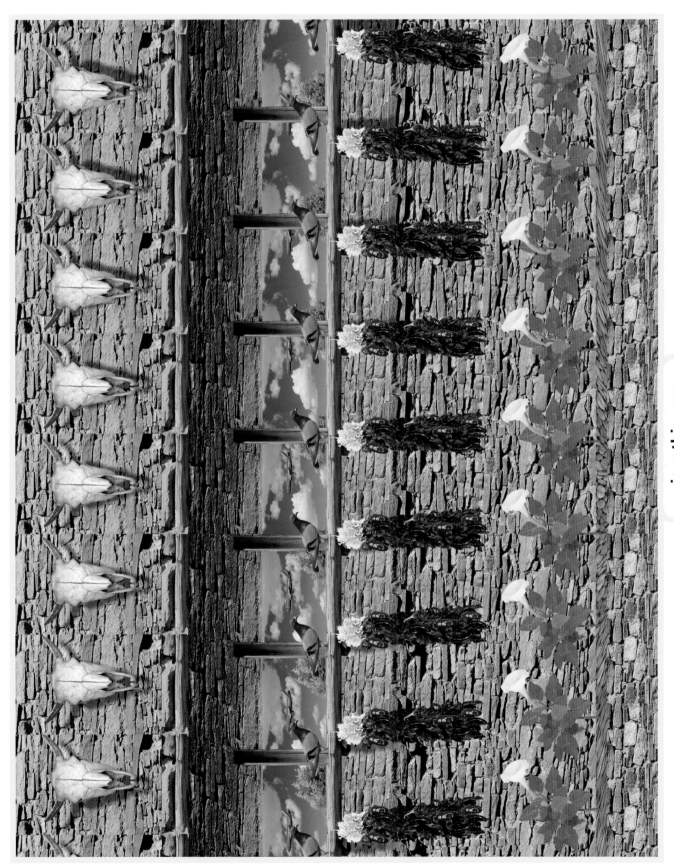

view this way

Pigeons

view this way

view this way

Waterfall

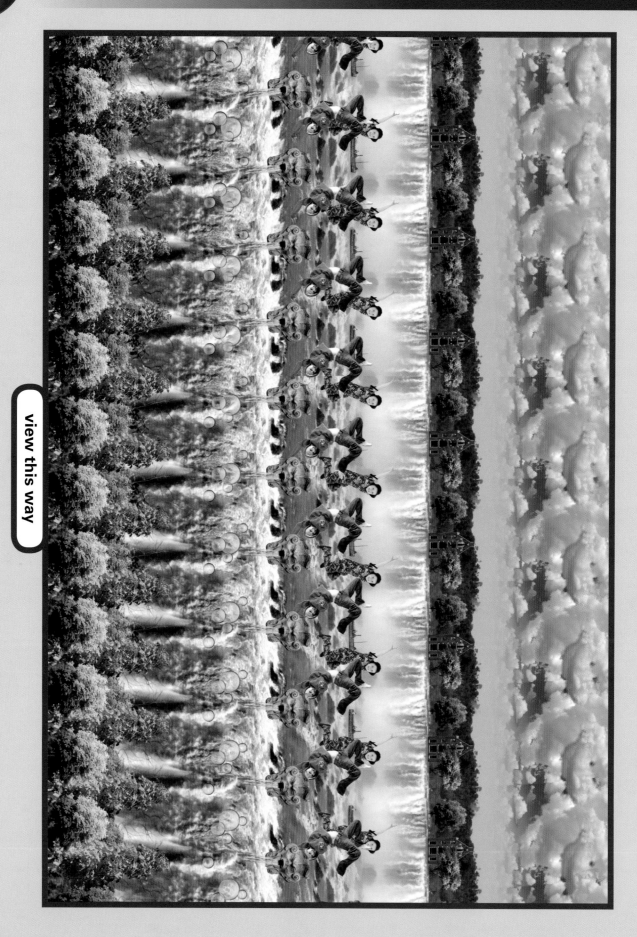

view this way

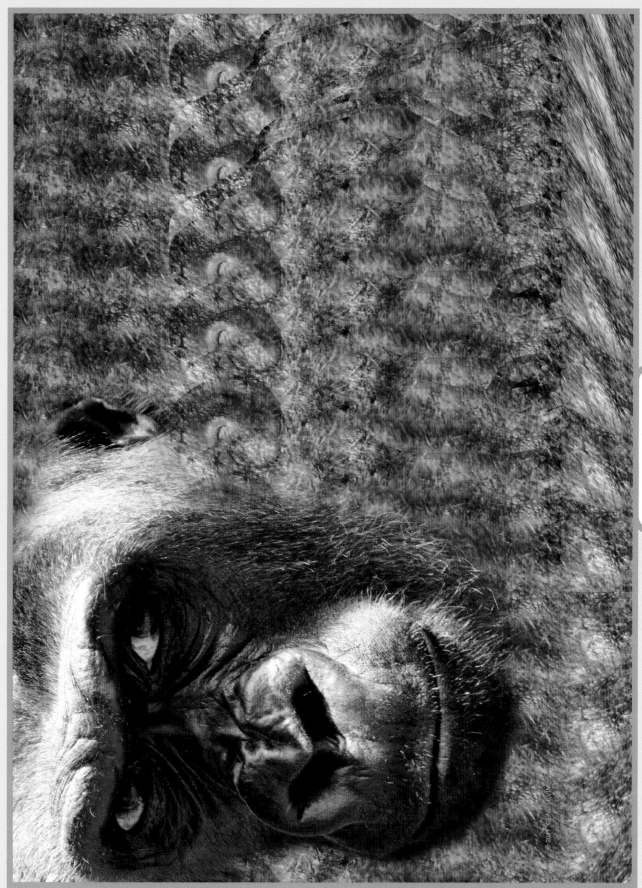

view this way

view this way

view this way

Sakura Pair

view this way

view this way

Pool Balls

view this way

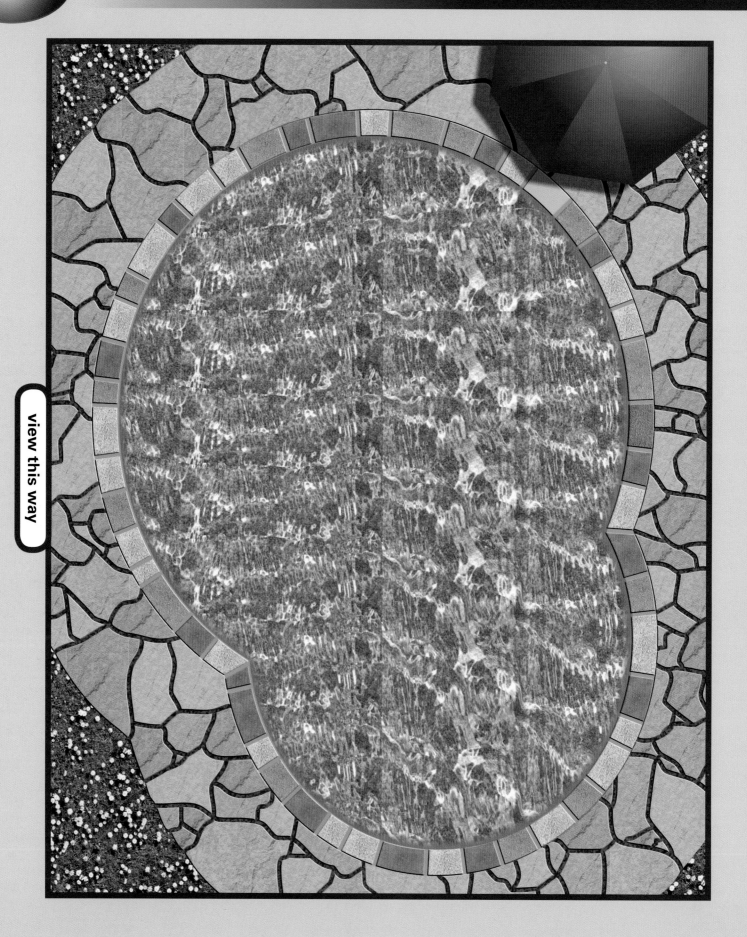

view this way

Dianthus

view this way

view this way

Rhino

view this way

© 2011 GENE LEVINE

Prohibitions

view this way

view this way

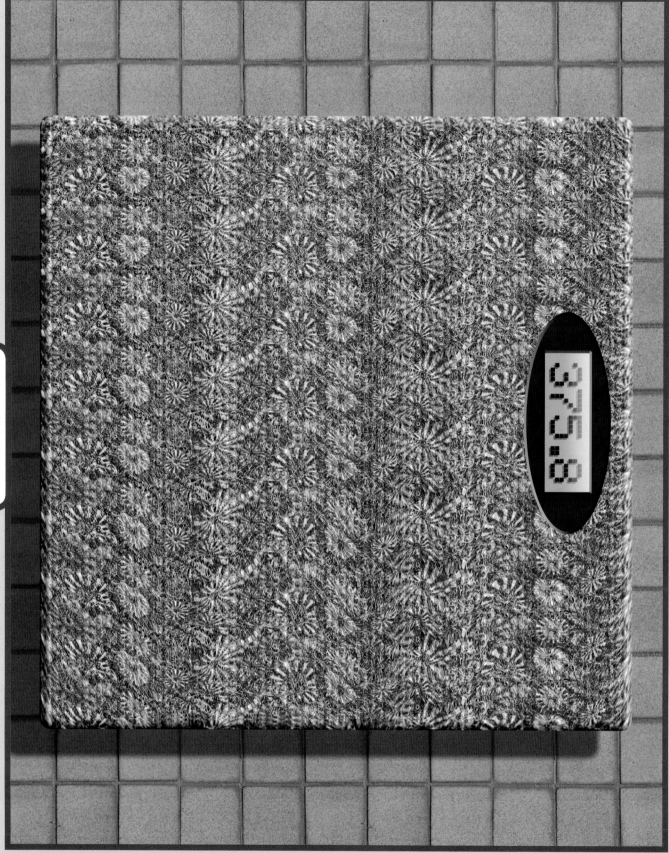

view this way

view this way

Snow Person

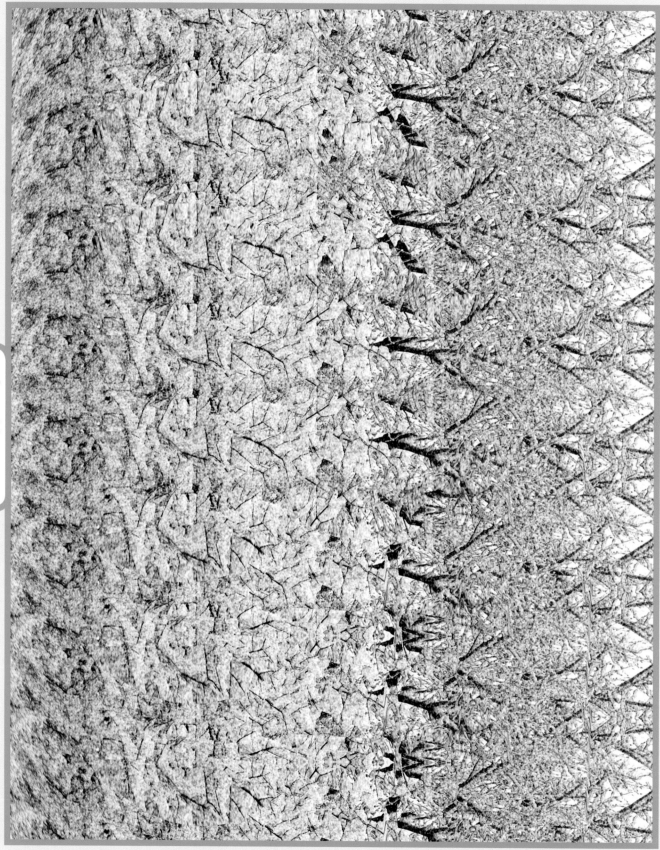

view this way

Bubble Man

view this way

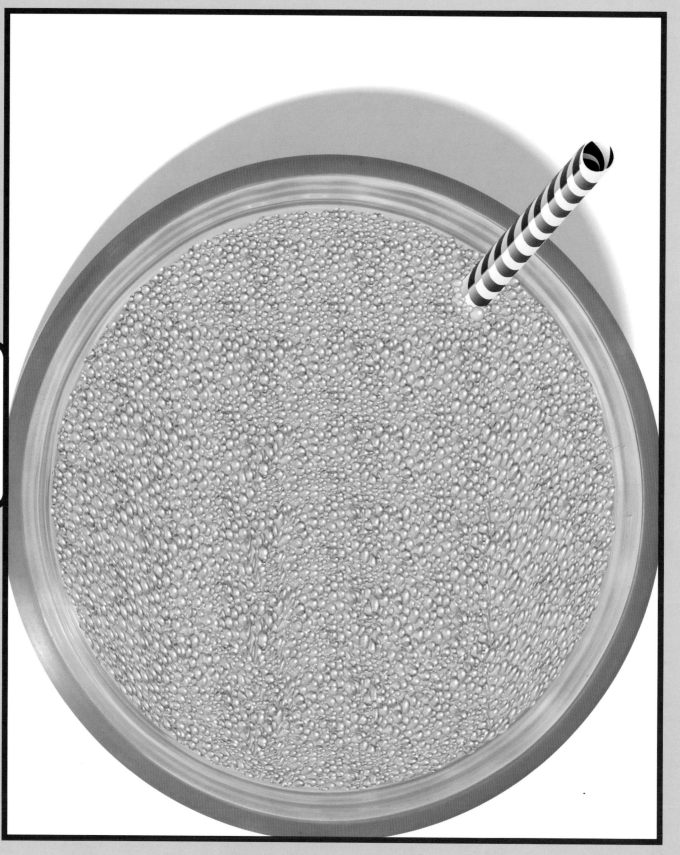

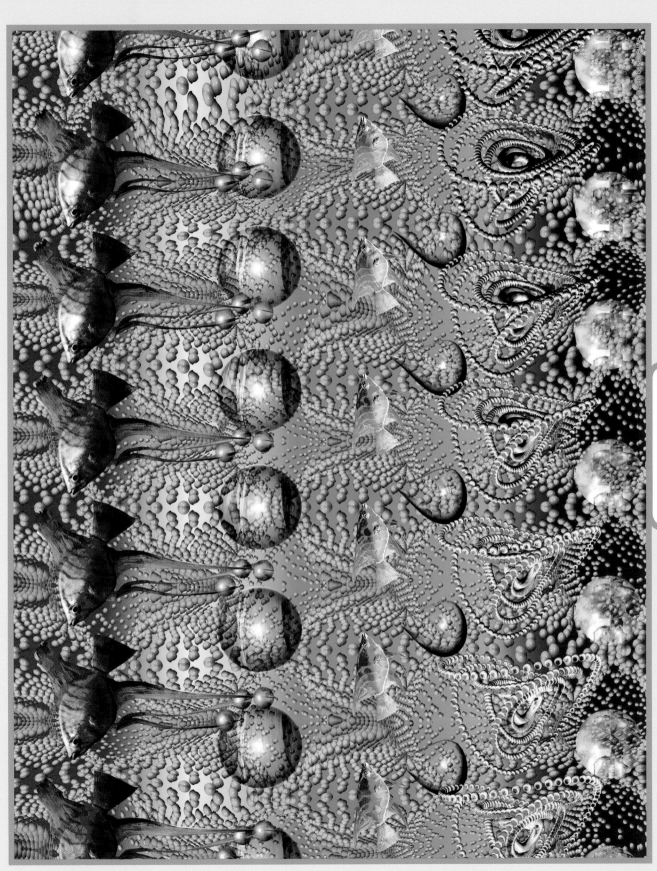

Floating Menagerie

view this way

view this way

Malbork Castle

view this way

view this way

The Park

view this way

view this way

Pharaoh

view this way

© 2011 GENE LEVINE

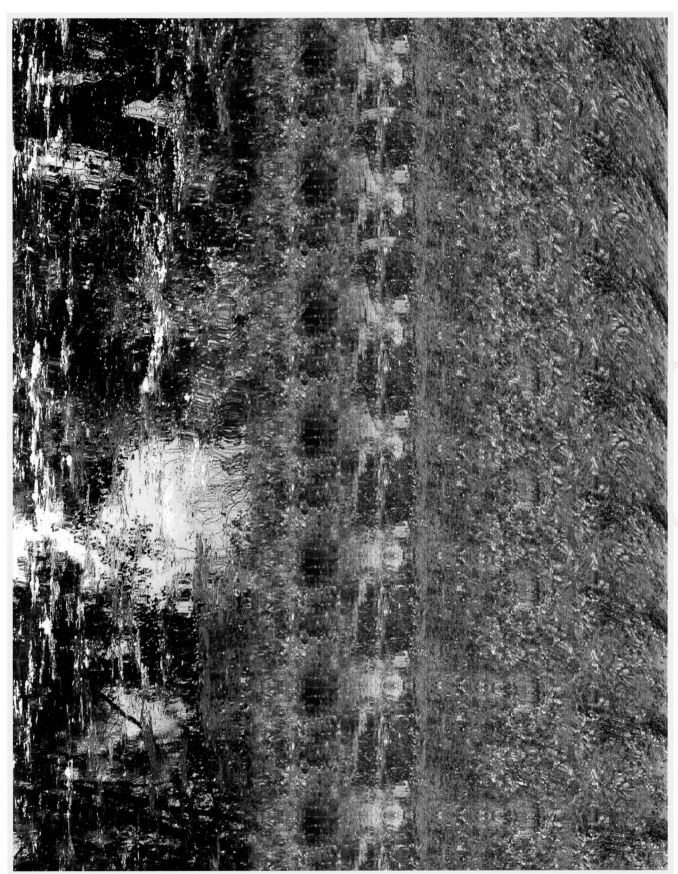

view this way

Hedgehog

view this way

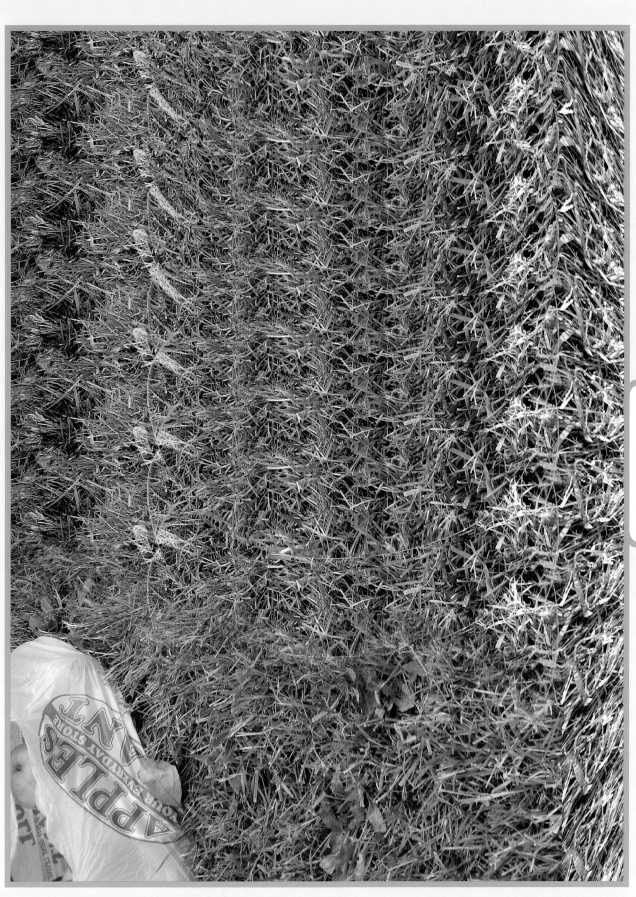

view this way

Surveillance

view this way

view this way

Bullet Train

view this way

view this way

Horse

view this way

view this way

Bounce

view this way

view this way

Bear River

view this way

Stereogram Reveals

Page 6 **Them Apples**

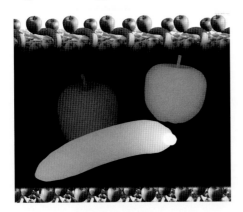

Page 10 **747 Emerging**

Page 11 **Magnifying Glass**

Page 12 **Green Man**

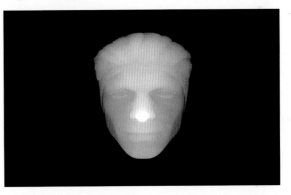

Page 13 **Clos la Madeleine**

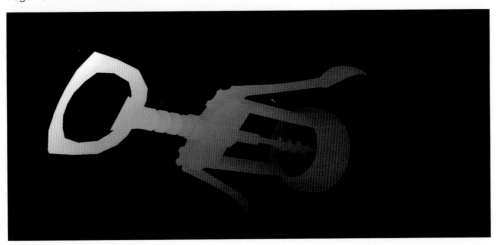

Stereogram Reveals

Page 14 **At Last**

Page 15 **Pyramids**

Page 16 **Lawn Chair**

Page 17 **3Discovery**

Page 18 **High Rise, High Maintenance**

Page 19 **Buddha Mountain**

Page 20 **Magical Cube**

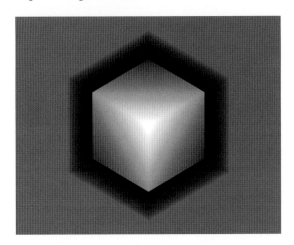

Page 21 **China**

Stereogram Reveals

Page 22 **Chaparral**

Page 23 **Joel's Vineyard**

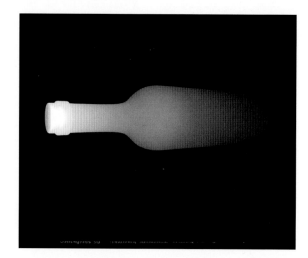

Page 24 **Baba's Sunflower**

Page 25 **Lighthouses**

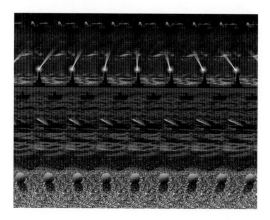

Page 26 **Blue Cove**

Page 27 **Western Windows**

Page 28 **Medicine Cabinet**

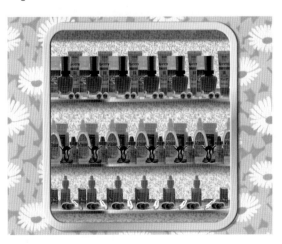

Page 29 **Green Tea**

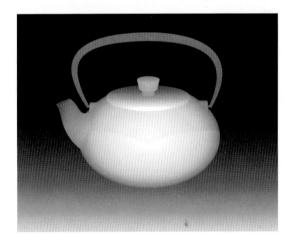

Stereogram Reveals

Page 30 **Dragon Wings**

Page 31 **Oscilloscope**

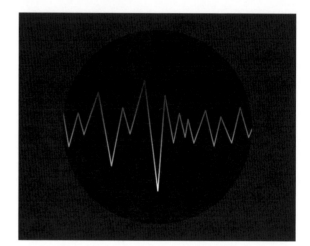

Page 32 **Palm Chair**

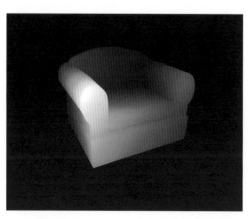

Page 33 **3D Express**

Page 34 **Snow People**

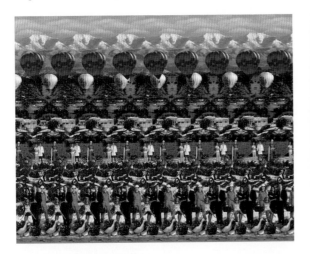

Page 35 **Eggs for Peace**

Page 36 **Dishwasher**

Page 37 **Robins**

Stereogram Reveals

Page 38 **Sandbox**

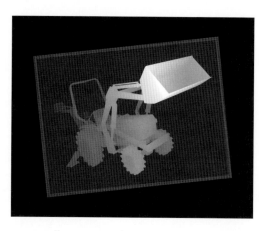

Page 39 **Dromedary**

Page 40 **Skateboarder**

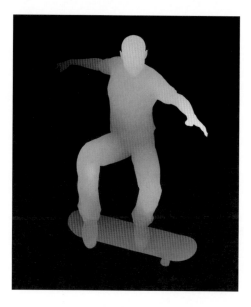

Page 41 **Show Horse**

Page 42 **Snowscreen**

Page 43 **Ocean Courtyard**

Page 44 **Field Compass**

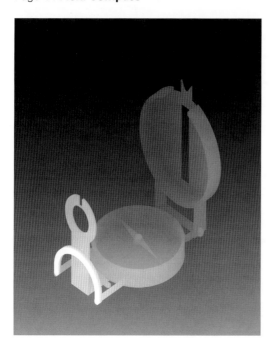

Page 45 **Locked**

Stereogram Reveals

Page 46 **Tea Pot**

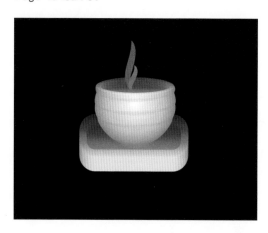

Page 47 **Wine Bar**

Page 48 **Fossil Mountain**

Page 49 **Stone View**

Page 50 **Underwater Danger**

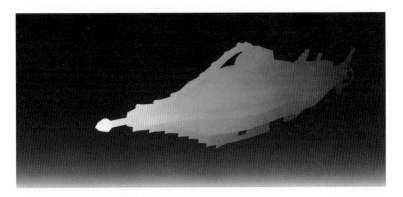

Page 51 **Stereo Sound**

Page 52 **Yellow Hills**

Page 53 **End of the World**

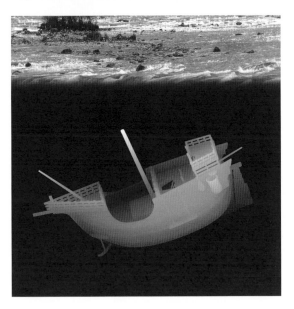

Stereogram Reveals

Page 54 **Stained Glass**

Page 55 **The Clock Inside**

Page 56 **Wine Barrel**

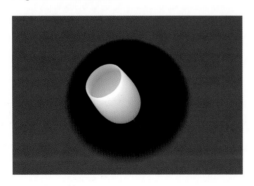

Page 57 **Athene Parthenos**

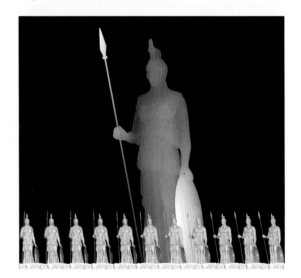

Page 58 **Sands of Time**

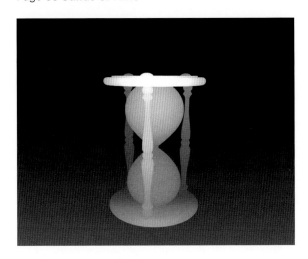

Page 59 **Elephant Wall**

Page 60 **Jack**

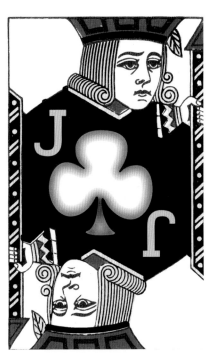

Page 61 **Equus Sacratissimum**

Stereogram Reveals

Page 62 **Flamingo Park**

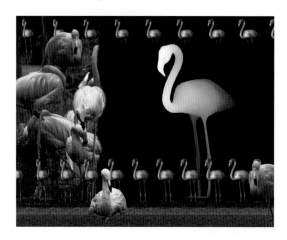

Page 63 **Southwestern Scene**

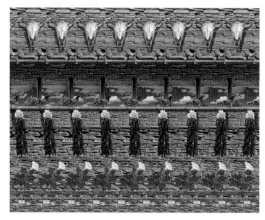

Page 64 **Pigeons**

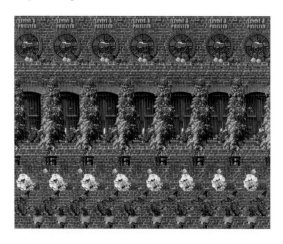

Page 65 **Glass Guitar**

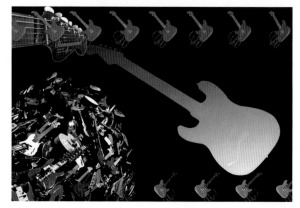

Page 66 **Waterfall**

Page 67 **Gorilla**

Page 68 **Hot Air Show**

Page 69 **Water Fantasy**

Stereogram Reveals

Page 70 **Sakura Pair**

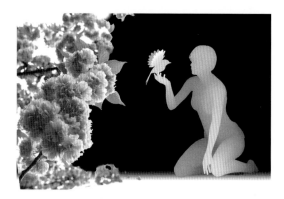

Page 71 **Sphinx**

Page 72 **Pool Balls**

Page 73 **Motorcycle**

Page 74 **Dianthus**

Page 75 **Levine Industries**

Page 76 **Rhino**

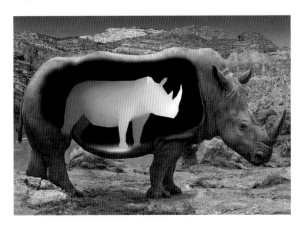

Page 77 **Water Tower (H$_2$0)**

Stereogram Reveals

Page 78 **Prohibitions**

Page 79 **The Choir**

Page 80 **Tipping the Scales**

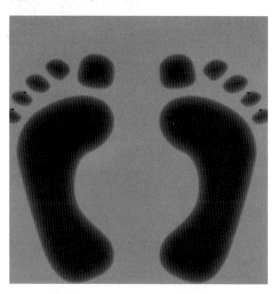

Page 81 **Sheep Farm**

Page 82 **Snow Person**

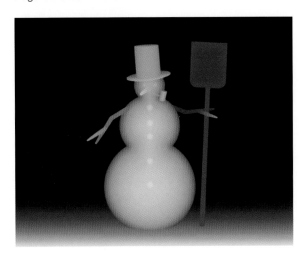

Page 83 **Lying Lion**

Page 84 **Bubble Man**

Page 85 **Rainbow Aquarium**

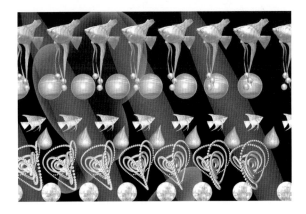

Stereogram Reveals

Page 86 **Floating Menagerie**

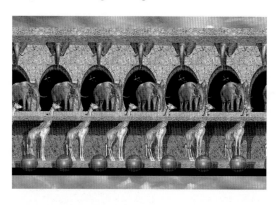

Page 89 **Heart of the Cactus**

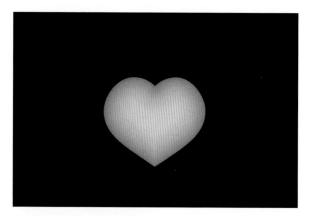

Page 87 **Mountain Eagle**

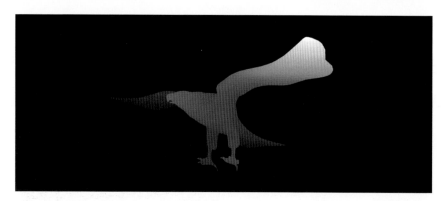

Page 88 **Malbork Castle**

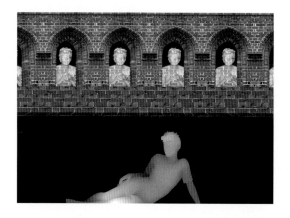

Page 90 **The Park**

Page 91 **Downward Dog**

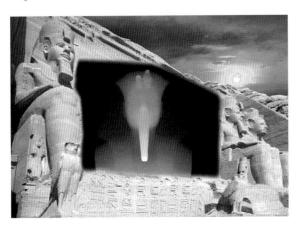

Page 94 **Hedgehog**

Page 92 **Pharaoh**

Page 95 **Fruit**

Page 93 **Bottom Feeder**

Stereogram Reveals

Page 96 **Surveillance**

Page 99 **Happy Cereal**

Page 97 **Plane Tree**

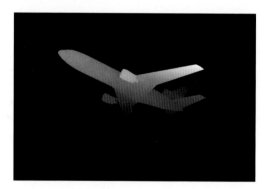

Page 100 **Horse**

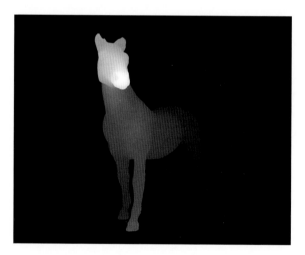

Page 98 **Bullet Train**

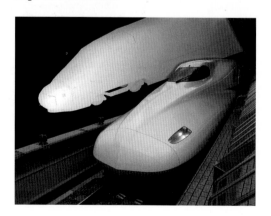

Stereogram Reveals

Page 101 **Mountain Warrior**

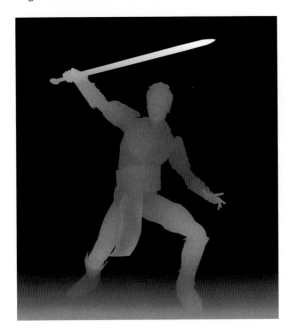

Page 102 **Bounce**

Page 103 **Deep Sea**

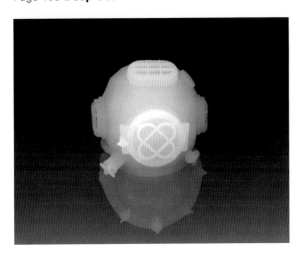

Page 104 **Bear River**

Stereogram images page by page

Other Stereogram publications by Gene Levine & Gary W. Priester

Eye Tricks – from Arcturus Publishing, 2004

Hidden Treasures – from Sterling Publishing (Barnes & Noble), 2008

Startling Stereograms – from Imagine Publishing, 2012

Philippine Edition of *Eye Tricks* – Dec. 2005

iPad Apps The Apple iTunes Store 2010

Eye Ball 3D Stereograms

Eye Ball 2 3D Stereograms

How to Eye Ball 3D Stereograms (Free App)

Stereogram book series from Takarajimasha, Japan
TJ Mook 1 June 2001
TJ Mook 2 Nov 2001
TJ Mook 3 June 2002
TJ Mook 4 Feb 2003
TJ Mook 5 June 2003
TJ Mook 6 Nov 2003
TJ Mook 7 Feb 2004
TJ Mook 8 Sept 2004
TJ Mook 9 Mar 2005
TJ Mook 10 Sept 2005
TJ Mook 11 May 2006
TJ Mook 12 Mar 2007
TJ Mook 13 Aug 2007
TJ Mook 14 Mar 2008

TJ Mook 15 Nov 2008
TJ Mook 16 Aug 2009
TJ Mook 17 June 2010
TJ Mook 18 June 2011
Mini-Mook 1 Feb 2004
Mini-Mook 2 Oct 2004
Mini-Mook 3 Nov 2005
Mini-Mook 4 Oct 2006
Mini-Mook 5 Nov 2007
Mini-Mook 6 Nov 2008
Mini-Mook 7 Aug 2009
Mini-Mook 8 June 2011
Mook plus CD Dec 2002
Best of Mooks Dec 2005
Best of: 2007 Calendar
Budget Mook 3 2009

Best Flowers Feb 2010
Budget Mook 1   2010
Best of Landscapes 2012

Stereogram book series from Thinkingdom, China
10 editions released 2011 and 2012

Kadokawa Publishing - Taiwanese dual stereogram series for Chinese markets
3D #1 July 2003
3D #2 Aug. 2003

Korean Edition from Nexus Publishing – Dec 2002